In The Darkest Moments

Deshay Williams

Title/Copyright Page

In The Darkest Moments

Published by: Books by L Mason: "A Safe Place"
P. O. Box 1162
Powhatan, VA 23139

Author: Deshay Williams
Cover Design: Canva

xoxoluv.shay@icloud.com

ISBN- 978-1-967205-31-8
LCCN: 2026930777

Printed in the United States of America

Table of Contents

Part Two Continued

INTRODUCTION

*I*n the darkest moments, we find the spark that fuels our survival. This powerful collection of poetry is a testament to the human spirit's capacity to overcome even the most daunting challenges. With raw emotion and unflinching honesty, these pages chronicle the journey from struggle to triumph, from brokenness to wholeness.

Through the lens of love, loss, and resilience, these poems remind us that our scars do not define us; instead, they represent our strength, courage, and determination to rise above. This book is a beacon of hope for anyone who has faced adversity and emerged stronger, wiser, and more radiant.

PART ONE

Hope

Sea of Pressure

A weight presses down, a crushing tide

A sea of pressure, that's hard to hide

The air is thin, the space is small

A trapped and helpless feeling, that's hard to stall

The walls are closing in, the ceiling's low

A sense of panic, that's hard to let go

The breath is short, the heart is racing fast

A desperate longing for a way to escape at last

The world's a distant hum, a muffled sound

A feeling of being, trapped and bound

The thoughts are screaming, the body's on fire

A primal urge to break free and desire

The pressure builds, the tension's high

A breaking point, that's hard to deny

The air is running out, the darkness closes in

A desperate cry for a lifeline to begin

But still I search for a glimmer of light

A way to break free, to shatter the night

I'll find my strength, I'll find my voice

A warrior's cry that echoes through this choice

The suffocating weight, it won't define

A heart that's strong, a spirit that's mine

I'll rise above, I'll fine my way

A breath of fresh air, a new dawn's ray

Cage of Fears

A prison of my own, a cell so tight

A cage of fears, a lock that's hard to fight

The walls are closing in, the air is thick

A trapped and helpless feeling, that's hard to kick

The doors are shut, the windows sealed

A world outside moving, while I'm revealed

The noise is muffled, the light is dim

A life on pause, while I'm stuck within

The thoughts are screaming, the heart is racing

A desperate longing for a way to keep pacing

The minutes tick by, like hours so slow

A trapped and restless soul, losing its glow

The keys are lost, the code is unknown

A life on hold, while I'm trapped in this zone

The world is moving, while I'm stuck in place

A feeling of suffocation that's hard to erase

But still I search for a glimmer of light

A way to break free, to shatter the night

I'll find my strength, I'll find my voice

A warrior's cry that echoes through this choice

The chains are heavy, the lock is strong

But I'll keep searching, I'll find my way back

I'll rise above, I'll break the mold

A spirit unbroken that refuses to be cold.

A Crushing Burden

A weight upon my chest, a pain so real

A burden crushing, a heart revealed

The tears fall like rain, the sorrow's a sea

A suffering so deep, it's hard to breathe, hard to be

The nights are darkest, the shadows loom

A relentless ache, a heart consumed

The world's a distant hum, a muffled sound

A soul so weary, it's lost its ground, lost its round

The memories linger, the scars remain

A painful reminder of joy that's in vain

The loss is palpable, the grief is raw

A heart so broken, it's hard to draw, hard to claw

The days are endless, the nights are cold

A suffering so profound, it's hard to hold

The weight of the world, it's crushing me

A fragile existence, a life that's barely free, barely see

But still I hold on to a glimmer of hope

A light in the darkness, a way to cope

I'll rise above, I'll find my way

A journey through suffering, to a brighter day, a new sway

The scars will remain, the memories stay

But I'll learn to heal, to find my way

I'll rise above, I'll find my voice

A heart that's broken, will learn to rejoice, will find its choice

Landscape of Scars

A body that's mine, yet feels so foreign too

A landscape of scars, a map of what I've been through

The diagnosis whispered, a life-altering phrase

A world that's shifted, where I struggle to find my place

The days are foggy, the nights are long

A constant reminder of what's gone wrong

The meds are a routine, a ritual to follow

A fragile balance between pain and shallow

The world outside moves at a pace so fast

But I'm stuck in slow motion, struggling to last

The simplest tasks, A Herculean feat

A body that's failing, a mind that can't retreat

The appointments and tests, a never-ending grind

A medical merry-go-round, where answers are few and thin

The specialists and experts, they all have their say

But I just want to feel like me, not a condition to display

But still I rise, with a heart that's strong

A warrior's spirit, that won't be wrong

I'll take each day, with a step that's slow

A journey of acceptance, where I'll learn to grow

The scars will remain, the memories linger on

But I won't let them define me, I'll rise above the pain

I'll find my own way, through the dark and the light

A life that's mine, with a heart still fighting, still igniting

Whisper

A nagging whisper, a persistent hum

A dripping faucet that won't succumb

A thought that echoes, a feeling that clings

A battle in my mind, where the war never ends, it stings

The doubts and fears--- they swirl, and they spin

A vortex of worry that pulls me within

The *'what-ifs'* and *'maybes'*, they taunt, and they tease

A relentless drumbeat that refuses to cease --- it's a disease

But I grab my shield, I raise my sword

A warrior's stance against the mental horde

I breathe deep, I focus on the ground

A fleeting calm in this never-ending round--- it's a sound

The tease of uncertainty, it's a wicked game

A constant whisper that I'm not quite the same

But I refuse to play, to give in to the fear

A spark of defiance that keeps me standing here, it's
clear

The battle's far from over, the war's not done

But I'll rise each time, like the morning sun

I'll face the foe with a heart that's bold

A warrior's spirit that will never be cold, it's told

The tease of doubt, it will always be there

But I'll learn to dance with the uncertainty, I'll show I
care

I'll find my strength in the fire that burns

A battle-hardened heart that yearns to learn and to turn

Clawed

A shadow once consumed me, a darkness I couldn't shake

A weight that pressed upon me, a chain that I'd mistake

The world was a blur, a haze of pain and despair

A constant craving, a voice that whispered "one more time --- just don't care"

But I fought the urge, I clawed my way up

A journey of setbacks, of trial and error, of giving up

The road was long and winding, the path unclear

But I held on to hope, a glimmer that I could persevere

The days were dark, the nights were long

A battle raged inside, a war that was wrong

But I found my strength in the fragments of my soul

A will to survive, to break the chains and make it whole

The first step was hard, the next was even more

A fragile thread of courage that I had to explore

But with each small victory, I found my voice

A whisper of triumph, a heartbeat that rejoiced

The scars remain, the memories linger on

A reminder of the fight, the struggle, and the dawn

But I'm not defined by my past, I'm free to be

A phoenix risen, a warrior, wild and carefree

Today I stand tall, a survivor of the night

A testament to hope, a beacon in the light

The addiction's gone, the chains are broken and cold

And in it's place, a love for life, worth more than gold

Constant Hum

A relentless foe, a constant hum

A whisper in my ear, a nagging drum

A battle rages with no end in sight

A war of wills where I fight to hold tight

The doubts creep in like thieves in the night

A voice that whispers, "you're not enough,

you'll never make it right"

The fears arise like a tidal wave

A crushing weight that threatens to engulf and cave

But I stand firm like a rock in the sea

A warrior's stance against the tide of anxiety

I breathe deep, I hold my ground

A fleeting calm in this never-ending round

The tease of uncertainty, a constant refrain

A reminder of vulnerability, a strain on my brain

But I refuse to yield, to let it consume

A spark of defiance that keeps me from being undone

The battle's far from over, the war's not won

But I'll rise each time, like the morning sun

I'll face the foe, with a heart that's bold

A warrior's spirit that never will be cold

The tease of doubt will always linger near

But I'll learn to dance, with the fear

I'll find my strength in the fire that burns

A battle-hardened heart that yearns to learn

Spectator of Life

A solitary figure in a crowded space

A heart that's locked with an invisible face

The walls are high, the bridges burned

An island unto myself where no one can learn

The silence is deafening, the noise is loud

A cacophony of thought that echoes and crowd

I try to escape, but it's all in vain

A prisoner of my own in this isolating pain

The world outside moves with a rhythm and beat

But in my world, there's just a hollow repeat

I watch from the shadows, a spectator of life

A longing to connect, but it's just a distant strife

The words unspoken, the feelings untold

A heart that's heavy with secrets to hold

I try to reach out, but my hand is stayed

A fear of rejection, that's always displayed

But even in the darkness, there's a spark of fire

A flame that flickers with a desire to connect and aspire

It's a tiny voice that whispers low and sweet

A reminder that even in isolation, I'm not completely beat

Clouded with Tears

A piece of me is gone, a void remains

A hollow in my heart, where love used to sustain

The echoes of memories, they still linger on

But the silence is deafening, where your voice is gone

The world outside moves, with a pace so fast

But time stands still, in this moment of loss that's cast

I search for answers in the eyes that remain

But they're clouded with tears, and a grief that's in vain

The memories of you, they still shine so bright

A bittersweet reminder of a love that's lost its light

I'll hold on to the laughter, the tears, and the fights

But it's just not the same without you here tonight

The days are long, the nights are cold

A loneliness that settles, like a story that's been told

I'll wander through the house, with a heart so sore

Searching for a glimpse of the one I love no more

But I know you're gone, and I'll be okay

A heart that's broken will mend with time and pray

I'll hold on to the love that we shared in life

A memory that lingers, a love that cuts like a knife

I'll miss you more with each passing day

But I'll honor your memory in every way

Your love will live on in my heart and soul

A bittersweet reminder of a love that made me whole

A Million Faces

A million faces in a crowded room

A sea of strangers where I find no home

The walls close in, the silence screams

A loneliness that clings like a shadow's seams

I wear a mask, a fragile disguise

A shield to hide behind a forced surprise

I smile and laugh, I play the part

But deep inside, a heart beats with a lonely art

The city's noise, a distant hum

A reminder of the world that's gone numb

I walk alone, through empty streets

A ghost among the living, with no place to meet

The phone is silent, the message few

A longing for connection, with nothing to do

I try to reach out, but my voice is lost

A whisper in the darkness, with no one to count

The stars above, a distant twinkling show

A reminder of the vastness that I cannot know

I feel so small, so lost, and so alone

A tiny speck in a universe that's gone

But even in the darkness there's a glimmer of light

A spark within me that refuses to fade or fight

It's a tiny flame that flickers with hope

A reminder that even in isolation, I'm not a hopeless scope

Darkness and Joy

Life is a canvas, a messy art

A splash of colors, a work in progress, a beating heart

We paint the moments with strokes bold and fine

A masterpiece unfolding with every step and every line

The brushstrokes wild, the colors blend and sway

A dance of contrasts in life's crazy way

We add the shadows, we add the light

A portrait of moments where darkness and joy take flight

We mix the textures, we play the hues

A symphony of experiences where love is the muse

The canvas evolves with every choice we make

A work of art emerging for the heart's sake

Life is a canvas with space to create

A journey of moments where we participate

We add the colors, we shape the form

A masterpiece of life where love is the norm

In the end, it's not the perfection we seek

But the beauty of moments where love makes us speak

A life that's lived with a heart that's true

A masterpiece unfolding with moments made for you

Face the Fears

Life is a journey, a winding road

A path unwinding through mountains and load

It twists and turns with ups and downs

A journey of moments where joy and pain are found

The sun rises high, the stars shine bright

A canvas of wonder in the dark of night

We walk alone, we walk with friends

Through laughter and tears, life's story unfolds in trends

We chase the dreams, we face the fears

We live the moments through all the years

The breath we take, the heart that beats

A symphony of life where every moment's a treat

Life is a gift, with moments sweet

A dance of shadows where love and loss meet

We rise, we fall, we learn, we grow

A journey of moments where the heart does know

In the end, it's not the years in life

But the life in years that cuts like a knife

It's the love we share, the moments we seize

A life that's lived with a heart that breathes and frees

Moment's Breath

Life is a whisper, a fleeting breeze

A moment's breath, where memories are sneeze

It swirls and twirls like leaves in the air

A dance of time where nothing's quite fair

We chase the sunbeams, we hide from the rain

We weave through shadows in life's crazy game

The clock ticks onward, the moments slip away

A puzzle of now, where the heart has its say

We gather threads of joy and of pain

We stitch them together to make life's crazy gain

The colors blend, the patterns show

A tapestry of moments where love makes us go

Life is a spark that ignites and fades

A flash of now in the vastness of sades

It's what we do with the time we have here

A choice of how in life's fleeting year

In the silence, the heart whispers low, "live, love, breathe, and let the moments grow"

For life's a whisper, a breath in the night

A moment's magic where love is the light

Emptiness

Echoes of emptiness, a hollow space

A heart that whispers with a lonely pace

The words unspoken, the touch unfound

A silence that screams where love's supposed to be
around

I search the shadows for a loving glance

A fleeting touch, a moment's chance

But like sand between fingers, it slips away

Leaving me with nothing but a hollow day

The world outside moves with laughter and cheer

But in my heart there's just a hollow fear

That I'll forever search for a love that's mine

But like a ghost, it haunts me and leaves me behind

The nights are dark, the days are gray

A monochrome world where love's gone astray

I try to fill the void with moments and noise

But the emptiness remains, a heart that's lost its voice

Maybe someday the walls will crumble down

And love will find me in a gentle sound

Until then, I'll wander through this empty space

Searching for true love in this place

A Warrior's Roar

In the heat of the fight, I find my strength

A warrior's roar that echoes at length

The battle's fierce, the stakes are high

But I won't back down, I'll take my stand, and I won't die

The enemy's closing with a deadly pace

But I'll dig in deep and find my fighting space

I'll take each blow, I'll rise each time

For I am a warrior, and I won't give in, I'll make it mine

The war is raging like a stormy sea

But I'll rise above with a heart that's free

I'll take each wave, I'll ride the tide

For I am a warrior and I'll not be denied

I'll stand tall now with a spirit bold

I'll face the foe with a heart that's cold

I'll take the hit, I'll rise again

For I am a warrior and I'll make it through, I'll win

The battle's not won, but I'll take the ground

I'll fight for what's mine with a warrior's sound

I'll rise up strong, I'll make it clear

For I am a warrior, and I won't give up, I'll persevere

Doubts and Reflections

Shadows cast, a mirror's gaze

A reflection of doubts, in endless daze

Not enough, the whisper creeps

An echo that lingers, a heart that sleeps

The world outside, a vibrant hue

But inside, a void, a feeling "not true"

Comparisons swirl, a toxic tide

Drowning out the voice that's trying to be heard inside

But here's the thing, you're human, flawed, and fine

Your worth isn't defined by someone else's design

You are enough, in this messy, beautiful mess

A work in progress with strengths to express

The cracks and scars, they tell a story too

Of resilience, of trials, of moments made true

You're not alone, in these feelings grasp

We're all just figuring it out, as we clasp

So take a breath, let go of the *'not enough'*

You are enough in this moment, that's tough

A Haunting Echo

Lost in the haze of a love that's gone cold

A distant memory of a heart that's grown old

The whispers of love, they still remain

A haunting echo of a love that's lost its way, in vain

The bed is empty, the nights are long

A silence that screams with a heart that's been wronged

I search for the answers in the shadows that play

A longing to turn back to the love that slipped away

The heart is heavy with the weight of what's past

A love that's lost in the memories that won't last

I try to move on, to let go of the pain

But the heart remembers, and the love remains like a
refrain

The love we had, it was real and true

A flame that burned bright, but now it's just a memory
or two

I'll hold on to the love that we once shared

A bittersweet reminder of a love that's hard to leave
unrepaired and gone, but still so dear

Bittersweet Reminder

A love like ours, it doesn't fade

A memory that lingers, a heart that's been made

The echoes of laughter, they still remain

A bittersweet reminder of love's sweet refrain

The space you left, it feels so cold

A hollow in my chest, a heart that's grown old

I try to move on, to let go of the pain

But the heart remembers, and the love remains

The nights are dark, the days are gray

A world without you is a world that's gone astray

I search for answers in the eyes that I know

A longing to turn back to the love that we once knew
how

The heart is broken, the love is gone

A chapter closed where the story's been written wrong

But I'll hold on to the love that we once shared

A memory that lingers, a love that's hard to leave unrepaired

The love we had, it doesn't die

A flame that flickers, a heart that's still alive

I'll keep it burning, though the flame is low

A love like ours, it doesn't fade, it just lets go

A Chapter Closed

Love's ghost remains, a haunting presence here

A whisper in the night, a memory that draws a tear

The echoes of what we had, they still resound

A longing for what's lost, a love that's turned to ground

The space you left, it feels so vast

A void that aches with a loneliness that's hard to pass

I try to fill it with the memories we've made

But they're just reminders of the love that's been
betrayed

The nights are long, the days are cold

A gray horizon where our love used to unfold

I search for answers in the eyes that I know

A longing to turn back to the love that we once knew

The heart is heavy, the love is gone

A chapter closed where the story's been written wrong

But I'll hold on to the love that we once shared

A bittersweet memory that's hard to leave unrepaired

Front Lines

I'm on the front lines of a war that's been waged

A battle for my soul, a fight that's been engaged

The enemy's fierce, with a relentless might

But I won't back down, I'll stand and fight

The scars of the past, they still linger on

A reminder of would, that have left their mark, gone

But I rise above with a heart that's strong

A warrior's spirit that's determined to move on

I'll take each step with a courageous stride

I'll face the fear, I'll take the enemy's pride

I'll stand my ground with a heart that's true

For I know that I'll emerge with a victor's crew

The battle's raging, the stakes are high

But I'll hold on tight to the hope that's inside

I'll fight for what's mine, I'll claim my right

For I am a warrior, and I won't give up the fight

The war is long, the road is tough

But I'll rise above with a spirit that's rough

I'll take each blow, I'll rise each time

For I am a warrior, and I'll make it through and shine

A Shattered Mirror

The ache remains, a hollow space

A shattered mirror, reflecting a lost face

The fragments of love, they still remain

A bittersweet reminder of what was and what can't be gained

The memories linger like a haunting refrain

A bittersweet melody that plays in vain

I search for the pieces of a love that's gone

A puzzle incomplete, where the heart is torn

The nights are long, the days are gray

A monochrome world, where love used to sway

I try to move on, to let go of the pain

But the heart remembers, and the wound remain

The echoes of laughter, they still resound

A haunting whisper of a love that's lost its ground

I clench my fists, I hold on tight

But the memories slip into the dark of night

The heart is broken, the love is gone

A chapter closed, where the story's wrong

But in the silence, a spark will ignite

A flame of hope, that love will shine again-- in time

Weight of the World

Tried eyes, weary soul

Weight of the world taking its toll

The dreams you had now feel like dust

What's the point when it all feels like rust

The ache in your chest, it won't subside

Thoughts of giving up, they start to reside

Like a whisper in the dark, it's hard to shake

The feeling that you're just not enough for the weight
you've made

But here's the thing, you're not alone

In this struggle, you're not on your own

There's light in the dark, a flicker, a spark

A reason to hold on, to leave the dark mark

You're carrying weight, but you don't have to be defined

By the heaviness you're letting seep inside

You're strong, resilient, you're capable of more

Than you know, than you've seen, than this moment's
score

So, take a breath, let it out slow

Let the weight down, just for a moment, don't go

You're not giving up, you're just giving in

To the strength within that will see you through the night

A Burden Born

Empty halls, a hollow breeze

A silence that whispers secrets to the trees

A vacant chair, a missing piece

A space that's left for something to release

The echoes whisper of what's been lost

A memory lingers at the cost

Of time that's gone, of love that's past

A longing ache that will forever last

The emptiness is a heavy weight

A burden born in a quiet space

A search for answers in a hollow place

A yearning heart with an empty face

Yet in the stillness, a truth is found

A space that's empty can be filled with sound

A life that's hollow can be made anew

A heart that's broken can be remade true

The emptiness is a canvas wide

A space for dreams where hopes reside

It's a reminder, too, of what's to come

A chance to create a life that's begun

Empty Spaces

Empty spaces, hollow sound

A silence that echoes all around

A vacant gaze, a lost refrain

A search for meaning in an empty plain

The hours stretch, a barren land

A drought of thought, a hollow hand

The words are gone, the feelings fade

In an empty space where nothing's made

A blank page stares, an empty frame

A work of art that's yet to claim

A life unlived, a story untold

A search for purpose in an empty hold

The emptiness whispers, a haunting sigh

A reminder of what's yet to be

A call to create, to fill the space

To find the meaning in the empty place

The void is deep, the void is wide

But its center, a spark resides

A flame that flickers, a light that shines

A beacon in the emptiness that guides the way to design

Tough But True

Pain lingers like a shadow at night

But love and strength can be the morning light

Scars remain, but they're maps of where I've been

Proof that I've walked through fire and found my way
again

Tears fall like rain, but they also wash me clean

Each breath is a step forward, a chance to mend

In the dark, I found my inner spark

Now I rise stronger and let my spirit mark

I'm not the same, and that's okay

I've been broken, but I've learned to heal in a way

Pain was a teacher, tough but true

Now I use its lessons to see my future

P A R T

T W O

A Gentle Voice

In the mirror's gaze a shadow plays

A reflection of doubts in endless ways

A voice inside that whispers low

"You're not enough, you'll never make it grow"

The words cut deep, the fears take hold

A fragile self that's hard to unfold

A constant loop of what's wrong and what's lacking

A sense of worth that's forever shaking

I search for validation in others' eyes

A fleeting fix for a deep demise

I compare and contrast in a never-ending game

A feeling of inadequacy that's hard to tame

But in the silence a whisper speaks

A gentle voice that my heart seeks

"You're more than flaws, you're more than pain"

A truth that whispered like a love refrain

It's hard to hear, it's hard to see

The beauty in myself through the lens of insecurity

But I'll take a step, I'll take a breath

I'll find my worth in the depths of my being and leave

Panic

The earth above, it presses down

A weight that's crushing, a feeling of drown

The darkness closes, a suffocating space

A tomb of silence where I lose my place

I'm trapped inside with no way to flee

A prisoner of fear in a world that's not me

The sound of dirt, it falls like a drum

A beat that's counting the moments that are numb

The air is thick, the shadows loom

A sense of claustrophobia that's hard to consume

I'm searching for light, for a glimpse of the sky

But it's hidden away, and I wonder if I'll survive

The panic rises, the fear takes hold

A sense of losing control, a story untold

But in the depths, a spark burns

A flame of hope that my heart yearns

I'll clench my fists, I'll take a breath

I'll find my strength in this darkest depth

For even in darkness there's a way to rise

A chance to break free and open my eyes

Between the Light and Dark

The world's loud noise, it fades away

And night's whispers start in a gentle sway

Shadows dance upon the wall

A silent play of shapes that fall

The moon's pale beam, it casts a light

A path unwinds through the dark of night

In blackness deep the stars are born

A celestial show that's endlessly torn

Between the light and the dark's disguise

A cosmic dance, where mystery resides

The night's dark wings, they shelter dreams

A world of rest where worries scream

The darkness soothes with a calming hand

And leads you deep to a peaceful land

And when the dawn begins to break

And night's dark veil starts to unravel and shake

The light returns with its warm caress

And a new day dawns with its hopeful mess

Dark Wings

Night's dark wings, they softly fold

Around the world, a quiet hold

The day's loud din, it fades to hush

And stars appear like diamonds brushed

And shadows lap, the secret stay

Of things unseen in a hidden way

The wind whispers low through trees that sway

A lullaby that chases the day

The moon's pale light, it casts a glow

On paths unwind, where dreams begin to flow

Fear's sharp edge, it softens in the night

As darkness wraps a comforting sight

The world's loud voice, it grows still

As night's dark peace begins it work to fill

In blackness deep a spark resides

A beacon burns where hope abides

And when the dawn begins to creep

And the night's dark shadows start to sip

The light returns with this warm touch

And a new day waits with a gentle clutch

Tomb of Silence

The weight is crushing, the darkness deep

A suffocating grip that won't release its keep

The earth is piling, the sound of dirt on stone

A tomb of silence where my screams are overthrown

I'm trapped below with no escape in sight

A prisoner of shadows in an endless night

The pressure builds, the air is thin

A feeling of drowning where my lungs are pinned

The world above is distant and far

A memory fading like a dying star

I'm lost in the dark with no guiding light

A soul submerged in the depths of night

The weight is overwhelming, the fear is real

A sense of helplessness that's hard to conceal

But in the stillness, a spark remain

A flame that flickers, a light that won't wain

I'll hold on to it, I'll let it guide

A tiny beacon in the dark inside

For even in darkness there's a way to breathe

A chance to rise and find the surface and be free

In Blackness

Shadows fall like curtains wide

Darkness gathers a silent tide

The day's loud voice, it fades to gray

And night's whispers start in a soothing way

In blackness space expands

A world of dreams where secrets stand

Fear's cold touch, it loses grip

As stars above begin their quiet flip

The darkness breathes, a patient friend

Waiting for dawn when paths will mend

In its depths, a spark can choose

To guide you through to light's gentle muse

The city's hum, a distant sound

As night's cool air wraps all around

The trees lean in with leaves that sway

In a lullaby that chases the day

In darkness shadows play and hide

A game of shapes where fears divide

But stillness creeps with a calming hand

And leads you deep to a peaceful land

The night's dark waves, they gently rock

A lancing calm that smoothes the shock

Of all the day, in its blinding glare

Has brought to you, in joy or despair

And when the stars begin to fade

And night's dark reign is gently played

The darkness yields to morning's glow

And a new day dawns with its light to show

Around the World

Night's dark wings, they softly fold

Around the world, a quiet hold

The day's loud din fades to hush

And stars appear as diamonds brushed

In shadow's lap, the secrets stay

Of things unseen in a hidden way

The wind whispers low through trees that sway

A lullaby that chases the day

The moon's pale light casts a glow

On paths unwind, where dreams begin to flow

Fear's sharp edge, it softens in the night

As darkness wraps a comforting sight

The world's loud voice, it grows still

As night's dark peace begins its work to fill

In blackness deep, a spark resides

A beacon burns, where hope abides

And when the dawn begins to creep

And night's dark shadows start to seep

The light returns with its warm touch

And a new day wakes with a gentle clutch

Chains

Fear's heavy chains, they once did bind

A weight that anchored a heart and mind

The doubts crept in, the fears did grow

A darkness that seemed to have no end in show

But I reached for light, for a guiding star

A beacon that shone near and far

I breathed through the pain, I faced the night

And found my courage in the morning's first light

The fears still linger, they still remain

But I confront them now with a heart that's plain

I step into the unknown with a spirit bold

And let my strength be my story told

The chains are broken, the path is clear

A new horizon beckons, a future that's dear

I'm rising strong, I'm moving on

With a heart that's open and a spirit that's won

The shadows fade, the light takes hold

A new path unfolds where courage is my gold

I'm not held back, I'm not the same

For I've faced the fear and found my flame

Heart Sustains

Hollowed space, a silence reigns

A stillness that the heart sustains

A vacant gaze, a searching mind

A longing for what's left behind

The echoes whisper of memories past

A bittersweet reminder of love that's cast

A shadow falls across the ground

A sense of loss that's hard to sound

The emptiness is a heavy chain

A weight that's born through joy and pain

A search for meaning in a hollow place

A yearning heart with a searching face

Yet in the darkness, a spark is lit

A flame that flickers, a light that's hit

A chance to heal, to mend the tear

To find the beauty in the emptiness that's here

The space is hollow, but not bare

For in its depths, a story's waiting there

A tale of growth, of love and light

A journey through the dark of night

Wave Crash

Breathe, just breathe, the darkness fades

Panic's grip loosens, waves crash shades

Of calm return, heartbeat slows its pace

You're safe now in this quiet space

Thoughts like storms, they come and go

You ride the winds, learn to let it flow

Ground yourself, feel the floor beneath

You're strong, you're here, the panic breathes

It's okay to fall, it's okay to fight

You rise again in the morning light

Panic's loud, but you're louder still

Inhale peace, exhale the chill

You got this

Nobody SAID IT WAS EASY

Rewrite My Story

I was a page with words unspoken

A narrative tangled, emotions unbroken

But I picked up the pen, I started to write

I'm rewriting my story, taking back my light

The chapters of pain, I'll turn them around

I'll turn wounds into wisdom, I'll spin them sound

My voice is the ink, my heart's the page

I'm writing a story where I am brave

No more a victim, I'm the hero now

I'm breaking the cycles, I'm finding my vow

I'll rise above the noise, I'll shine my way

I'm rewriting my story every single day

Anchored in Me

I was lost at sea, waves crashing strong

But I found an anchor, I learned to belong

It's rooted in me, in my core, in my soul

I'm anchored in me, I'm finding my goal

The storms will come, the winds will howl

But I'll weather the waves, I'll make it my howl

I've got this anchor, it's steady and true

I'm anchored in me, that's where I'll see through

No more drifting, no more lost at sea

I'm grounded in myself, that's where I'm free

I trust my compass, I trust my heart

I'm anchored in me, and we'll make it far

Threads of Strength

I'm weaving threads of strength from the fibers of pain

A tapestry of resilience where my spirit's the stain

Each strand a story, each knot a lesson learned

A mosaic of moments where I've found

The threads are imperfect, like me, like you

But woven together, they create something true

A reminder that beauty's born from the breaks

And strength's not the absence of pain, but the will to make

I'm threading hope into the fabric of my soul

Weaving love into the spaces where I've felt control

Creating a life where I am free, where I am me

Where threads of strength become the life I choose to see

You can do this

Fragments to Masterpiece

I was broken pieces, shattered on the floor

But I picked up the shards and started to explore

I found beauty in the breaks, in the edges rough

I'm crafting a masterpiece from the fragments tough

The cracks tell stories of where I've been

Of trials and triumps of moments I've seen

I'm piecing it together with love and with care

Creating a life that's mine with fragments I declare

I'm not the same, and that's the art

I'm turning my scars into a work of heart

I'm the artist, I'm the one who decides

I'm turning fragments into a masterpiece inside

Bloom Where You Are

Plant me in the cracks, I'll find a way

Roots will dig deep, I'll make it my day

In the hardest soil, I'll find my groove

Bloom where I am, with petals that prove

Adversity's the rain, it's true

But it's also the spark that makes me break through

I stretch toward the light, I find my hue

In the mess, I find the beauty, too

I'm growing, I'm changing, I'm finding my voice

In the wild, in the cracks, I'm making some noise

Bloom where you are, that's where you'll thrive

Wherever life puts you, that's where you'll survive

Wild and Free

I let go of what held me back

And found my wings, now I soar on track

No longer tied to what's past

I'm wild and free, my spirit's vast

I chase the winds of change

I dance with uncertainty, I rearrange

My path's not linear, it's wild and true

I'm finding me, and that's where I thrive

No cages hold, no fears define

I'm breaking rules, I'm making my rhyme

I'm the author of my story now

Wild and free, that's where I allow

You are
ENOUGH

Phoenix Rising

From the ashes of my past, I rise anew

Like a phoenix born with wings to break through

The fire that tried to burn me, fueled my flight

Now I soar above where the winds of change ignite

I reclaim my story, I own my voice

No longer defined by the chains that made my choice

I melt the shackles, I shatter the mold

I rise with every breath, with every story I've told

My scars are constellations, maps to my soul

Proof that I've navigated, and made my heart whole

I'm learning to love myself, flaws and all

To let go of what's past and let my spirit stand tall

After the Storm

The storm raged on, like a beast unleashed

Tried to uproot me, tried to leave me crushed

But I weathered the winds, I stood my ground

And when the skies cleared, I found I'd turned around

The rain washed away the tears I'd cried

Left space for growth, for a newfound pride

The scars remain like a map of my past

But they're reminders of strength, of moments I'll last

I learned to dance in the rain, to find my beat

To let the storms shape me but not define my seat

I'm finding my voice, I'm learning to soar

In the calm, I hear my heart, and that's where I explore

Unravel and Rise

I was a knot, tangled and tight

But I unraveled the threads and found my light

I learned to let go, to release and unwind

Now I'm unraveling, and I'm starting to find

The threads of doubt, the strands of fear

I'm pulling them loose, I'm wending clear

I'm finding my way through the messy unwind

And rising up with a spirit that's aligned

Unravel and rise, that's what I'm doing

Letting go of what's holding, and my spirit's booming

I'm finding my voice, I'm finding my path

Unravel and rise, that's where I'm at

BE Strong

Enpowerment

You took something from me, but you didn't take my
voice

I reclaim my body, my story, my choice

The scars are mine, the healing's mine to own

I'm breaking free from shadows, I'm stepping into light

I was not the problem, I was not to blame

My worth wasn't yours to take, my power's not a game

I'm learning to love myself, to see my value shine

To take back control and let my spirit align

Healing's not linear, it's a journey, not a place

But with each step forward, I find my peaceful space

I'm not defined by what happened, I'm defined by how I
rise

I'm strong, I'm brave, and I'm learning to thrive

Mental Challenges

Mind's a maze, thoughts can be loud

Breathe deep, find calm, let the peace unfold

It's okay to struggle, it's okay to feel

Take it one step at a time, you'll start to heal

Reach out for help, don't walk alone

Talk about it, let the weight lift off your tone

Small wins are wins --- celebrate them

Every breath's a chance to start again

You're stronger than you think, you're not alone

You've got this, take it day by day

Healing's a journey, not a destination

Be kind to yourself, that's where growth happens

Moment's Scream

A stormy night, a moment scream

Echoes of pain, a heart's dark dream

Shattered trust, a wound so raw

A memory that clings, a heart that's law

The weight of what happened, it still remains

A heavy burden through joy and pain

The echoes whisper a haughting refrain

A reminder of vulnerability, a loss of controls strain

But in the darkness a light can shine

A chance to heal, to break the chain

Of pain that's held, of fear that's real

A path to rise to learn to feel

You are not defined by what happened then

You are more than the pain; you are a survivor, a warrior,
a friend

The wound may scar, but it doesn't have to bind

You can rise above and let love and strength unwind

just

Breathe

Prisoner of Words

I was lost in shadows where fears would play

A prisoner of words, a captive of dismay

But I found my voice, my strength, my light

I broke the chains and took back my night

Scars remain, but they're maps of my fight

Proof that I rose and turned my pain to might

I learned to love myself, to let go of the blame

To see my worth and rise above the shame

You don't define me, your words don't control me

I'm free now, my spirit's taking flight

I heal with each step, with each new day

And in my strength, I'll mine my own way

Flame That Flickers

A hollowed shell, a vacant core

A space that's empty asking for more

The winds of change, they whisper low

Of memories lost and love that won't grow

The echoes remain of laughter and tears

A bittersweet reminder of all the years

The photographs, the stories untold

A sense of longing that never grows old

The emptiness is a canvas wide

A space for dreams where hopes reside

It's a reminder, too, of what's to come

A chance to create a life that's begun

In this hollow space, a spark can ignite

A flame that flickers, a light that guides

A path unwinds through the dark of night

A journey inward to a place of light

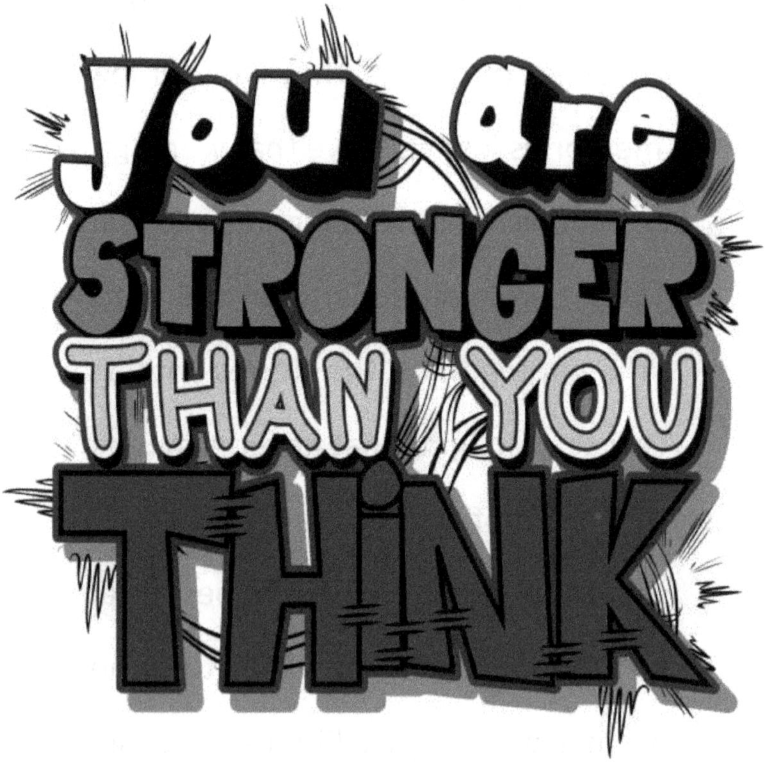
you are
STRONGER
THAN YOU
THINK

A Glowing Beacon

Darkness creeps, a shadow's sigh

The room is hollow, the lights say goodbye

In the black of night, fears take shape

But stillness waits for dawn's escape

Whispers in the dark, they come and play

Echoes of doubts, in endless gray

Yet in the depths, a spark remains

A beacon glows, and fear's chains break

Night's velvet shroud, it wraps me tight

A canvas for dreams where shadows take flight

In darkness, secrets hide and whisper low

But truth's ember flickers, and the night doesn't know

Darkness is a path where fears reside

But walk it bravely, and stars may guide

For in the black a spark can ignite

And lead you through to morning's gentle light

Puzzle Piece

I was a puzzle, broken into pieces

Each shard, a reminder of moments I'd freeze

But I picked up the fragments and started to mend

Found the strength to rebuild, to make my spirit
transcend

The cracks tell a story of where I've been

Of trials and tribulations, of moments I'd win

I weave the pieces back with threads of gold

Creating a mosaic of a story yet to unfold

I'm not the same, and that's the beauty found

In every break, a chance to grow, to spin around

My worth isn't defined by the breaks or the pain

But by how I rise, by the love I give and gain

I'm unbroken, I'm learning to thrive

With every step forward, I'm starting to jive

Push yourself
NO ONE IS GOING
TO DO IT
FOR YOU

A Love Unraveled

A heart unwinds like a threadbare rope

A love unraveled with a final stroke

The words are spoken, the bond is broke

A silence falls where love once awoke

The echoes linger of what we had found

A bittersweet reminder of moments lost and gone down

I search for the answers in the eyes that remain

A longing to turn back to love again

The space is empty, the bed is cold

A loneliness settles where love used to unfold

I try to fill the gap with memories and time

But the heart is hollow, and the love is lost in rhyme

The fragments of us, they still remain

A shattered dream, where love's refrain

I'll pick up the pieces, I'll mend the past

But the heart will ache until love comes at last

I can AND I will

Dawn Breaks

Shadows fade like the night before

A new dawn breaks on a heart that's more

The weight lifts off, the chains are gone

A sense of freedom in a spirit that's won

The memories linger like scars on the skin

A reminder of battles that I fought within

But I rise above, I let go of the pain

I find my strength in a heart that's whole again

I speak my truth, I claim my space

A voice that's loud in a world that's got it's pace

I'm not the same, I'm not that kid

I'm a survivor with a heart that been lit

The bully's words, they lost their sting

Or I found my worth in the heart's sweet ring

I'm rising strong, I'm moving on

With a spirit fierce and a heart that's won

The shadows fade, the light takes hold

A new chapter unfolds with a heart that's bold

I'm not afraid, I'm not alone

Or I faced the fear, and I've made it home

Words Cut Deep

The words cut deep, the scars remain

A painful memory that's hard to explain

The echoes of taunts, the laughter, and the pain

A weight that's not lingered like a constant refrain

The bully's voices, they still ring true

A reminder of fears that I once knew

But I rise above, I shake off the shame

I find my strength in a heart that's not the blame

I break the chains, I let go of the hurts

I find my voice in a world that's not so curt

I choose to heal, I choose to be free

I rise above like a phoenix --- meant to be

The scars remain, but they tell a tale

A story of strength, of a heart that's strong and hale

I'm not defined by the words they said

I'm defined by courage in the heart of my head

I walk tall with my head held high

A survivor's pride in a spirit that won't die

The bully's words, they no longer sting

For I've found my voice, and my heart's on the wing

Stream of Doubts

A voice inside, a constant hum

A critic's whisper that's hard to numb

A stream of doubt, a tide of fears

A sense of inadequacy throughout all my years

I measure myself against an endless scale

A standard high that's hard to prevail

I focus on flaws, on every single part

A sense of worth that's lost in my heart

The words echo loud, a relentless beat

A reminder of shortcomings, a constant repeat

I'm searching for proof, for a reason to be

A validation that's hard to see

But in this stillness, a spark ignites

A flame of selfworth that shines with gentle light

You're more than flaws, you're more than mistakes

A truth that's spoken like love that's real and great

It's hard to break free from the chains of doubt

To find my worth in a world that's loud and rough

But I'll take a step, I'll take a breath

I'll find my voice and let my spirit breathe

The Shadows Tremble

In the depths of fear, a spark resides

A flame that flickers, a light that abides

A voice that's whispering, a gentle tone

Beckoning me forward to a place I've known

The path unwinds through the dark of night

A journey inward to a place of light

The shadows tremble, the fears subside

As I step into the unknown with a heart that's pride

The doubts arise, the *'what ifs'* scream

But I confront them now with a spirit that's keen

I breathe through the uncertainty, I let go of the pain

And find my strength in the heart's refrain

There's no longer fear, it's a wall that's high

But a stepping stone to a place I can fly

I'm not held back, I'm not afraid

Or I face the fear and found my way

The light grows brighter, the path is clear

A new horizon beckons a future that's dear

I'm rising strong, I'm moving on

With a heart that's open and a spirit that's won

Pressed Upon My Mind

Fear's dark shadows, they once did bind

A weight that pressed upon my mind

The doubts crept in, the *'what ifs'* loud

A paralyzing grip that held me down --- a heavy cloud

But I face the fear, the anxiety's tied

I stepped into the dark, and let my spirit ride

The waves crashed strong, the winds did howl and
scream

But I stood tall and let my courage be the beam

The fears still come, they still remain

But I confront them now with a heart that's plain

I breathe through the doubt, I let go of the strife

And find my strength in the depth of my life

The shadows recede, the light begins to shine

A new path unfolds where courage is the design

I'm not held, I'm not defined

By the fears that once made my heart confined

I rise above, I break the chains

A freedom found in the hearts refrains

The fears no longer hold me in the sway

For I face the dark and found my way

Velvet Shroud

Darkness gathers like a velvet shroud

A midnight's hush that's softly proud

The world's loud noise, it fades away

And night's whisper starts in a gentle sway

Shadows dance upon the wall

A silent place of shapes that fall

The moon's pale beam, they cast a light

A path unwinds through the dark of night

In blackness deep the stars are born

A celestial show that's endlessly torn

Between the lightness and the darkness disguise

A constant dance where my mistress resides

The night's dark wings, they shelter dreams

A world of rest where worry screams

The darkness soothes with a calming hand

And leads you deep to a peaceful land

And when the dawn begins to break

And night's dark veil starts to unravel and shake

The light returns with it's warm caress

And a new day dawns with it hopeful mess

Sought to Scorch

In midnight silence where shadows dance and play

A phoenix rising, born of trials day

The flames that sought to scorch and leave her gray

The storms that rage, the winds that howled and screamed

The weights that pressed, the tears that fell like rain

All conspired to crush, to leave her broken and drained

But she, a vessel, tempered, refined, remained

The ghost of doubt, the whispers of fear

The echoes of pain, the scars that still appear

All moving threads of tapestry so fine

A mosaic of strength, a hard --- that's divine

For every step that's taken, every fall that's made

A lesson learned, a truth that's been displayed

The rubble of what's past, the dust of yesterday

Becomes the foundation on which she stands today

The road ahead, a winding path unwinds

A journey through the darkness to the light that blinds

But she with eyes aflame with heart alight

Steps forward, unafraid, into the unknown sight

For she is the sum of all she's overcome

The fires proof, the storm's drum

A warrior fears a heart that's bold and free

A love that's strong, a spirit that's meant to be

So let the pass be passed, let go of the pain

For she's a work of art, a masterpiece in vain

A beauty born of trials, a heart that's gold

A love that's risen like the mornings unfold

In every breath, in every step, she finds her way

Through the darkness to a brighter day

And though the road behind may still be rough and gray

She walks on, unafraid, into a brighter and bolder day

About the Author,

by the Author

My name is Deshay Williams, and I am 18 years old. I was born and raised in Richmond, Virginia. As a young child, I loved reading and always told myself that I would become an author. I feel honored to accomplish this dream at such a young age.

I started writing poetry to express and spread positivity, and to help others get through difficult times. I love expressing my feelings through poetry. It's become a tool for me to escape, and it helps me clear my mind as I focus on never-ending, challenging life issues.

Additionally, I'm hoping this book of poetry raises awareness in communities across the land.

Deshay Williams, Dec., 2025

www.ingramcontent.com/pod-product-compliance
Lightning Source LLC
Chambersburg PA
CBHW071132090426
42736CB00012B/2106